Miriam O'Neal

The Body Dialogues

LILY POETRY REVIEW BOOKS

Copyright © 2019 by Miriam O'Neal

Published by Lily Poetry Review Books
223 Winter Street
Whitman, MA 02382

https://lilypoetryreview.blog/

ISBN: 978-1-7337683-5-1

All rights reserved. Published in the United States by Lily Poetry Review Books.
Library of Congress Control Number: 2019954714

Cover Design: Martha McCollough
Cover Art: Based on August Rodin's *Nude Figure on Hands and Knees,* collection Metropolitan Museum of Art

In loving memory of Teeny Lynch,
first reader, second mother, philosopher

My thanks to the following for their unswerving care and careful reading of the poems in progress: Dzvinia Orlowsky, Mary Kane, Barbara Siegel Carlson, and Lee English. Thank you as well, to my compassionate and insightful editors, Eileen Cleary and Christine Jones who helped with the final care-full polishing. And bless you, dear daughter-in-law, Lynn O'Neal, for always encouraging, always being ready to read, and always sharing the path.

ACKNOWLEDGEMENTS:

Thank you to the editors of the following journals, who originally published poems from this collection.

Able Muse, "Postcard, Vermont (Love on the Rocks c. 1898)"
Cathexis Journal, "Gender Studies"
Blackbird Journal, "Delivered," "House"
Lily Poetry Review, "The Little Lights"
Poems2Go, "Change", "Evensong"
Silver Needle Press, "Change"
The Guide Book, "Homesick," "Sex and the Soul (Sesso e l'Anima)"

Table of Contents

    I

3 Birth Day
4 Anima
5 Eating God
6 The Sister Doesn't Say
8 Felucca
9 Bottle Journal, End of Lent
10 Meditation on Common Ground
11 A Brief History
12 Gender Studies
13 Evensong
14 Field
15 How You Know Where You Are
16 Book Night
18 The Fold
19 Home Economics
20 Chi Lines After The Stroke
21 Farmed Out
22 The only time
23 House
24 Becoming
25 Daybreak In Truro
26 After Her Hip Replacement
27 Change
28 Breathing

    II

31 Water
32 Homesick
33 Sex And The Soul (Sesso e l'Anima)
34 Postcard, Vermont (Love on the Rocks c. 1898)

v

35 Analogy
36 Last Harvest
37 No, Don't Tell Me
39 The Kindness of Anecdotes
40 Swimming Lesson

III

45 Postcard, Sardinia
46 Reading Jastrun's Memorials: What the Darkness Said
48 We speak of women converted into poems by their men
49 Reading The Contraband of the Hoopoe
50 We Watch the International Space Station Fly Overhead
51 Yankee Swap
52 The Sudden Tremendous Weight
53 Conjugation
54 The Little Lights
55 Life Inside and Out: A Cento
56 *Notes*

The Body Dialogues

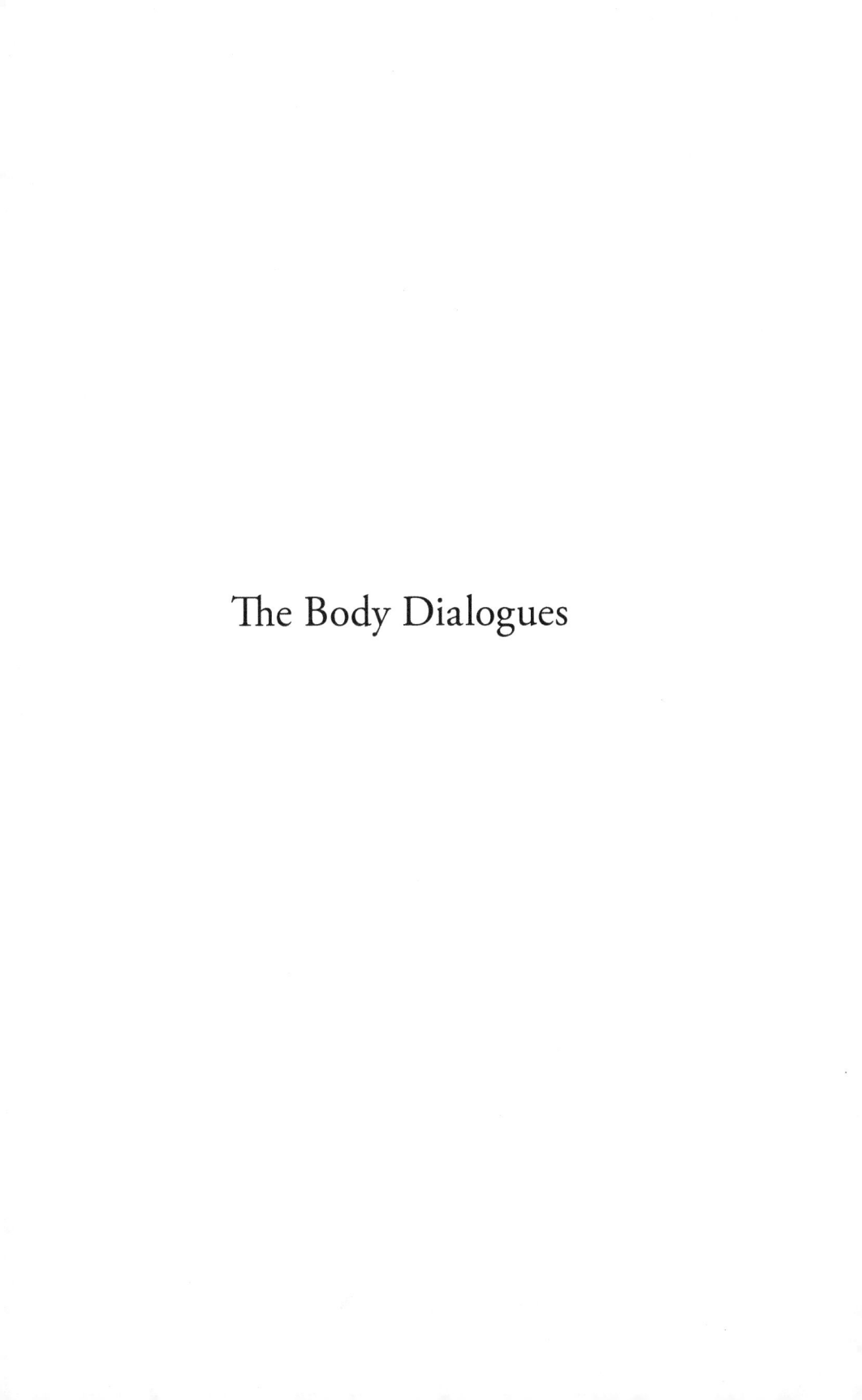

I

Birth Day

Already missing the weight of her lade,
she becomes an empty crib;

the burden of making
replaced by space.

If she is lucky
the child slides
like a christened ship,
to waiting waters

and loosed like the bottle's
broken neck, her body pours
what's left
into attending hands.

Anima

Across from Karbott's Farm.
The creek that fed the bog.

Tips of willow limbs trapped in snow—
a gurgle beneath the ice

like the chortle in a baby's throat
before she has words.

Knees wet after drinking from a skate-hacked hole,
mouth burned inside with cold, lips cracked.

Safe from hockey's slapped pucks,

from skating-skirted girls
who chip with toe picks to show

how they can twirl.
Heaven is anywhere alone

and close to water—
its lovely guttering.

I remember my hands as paws.

Eating God

Sometimes I am hungry for God,
but only when rain dimples the harbor

and ducks rocket through the slant
where light glances off the marsh grass

as if, somewhere, we had sun.

Then, I am hungry for the word
that tastes like the roof of the world.

In childhood I'd stand
at the communion rail,

my lips shaping the prayer my mother
taught me—then kneel to pray.

I'd gaze at the rafters when
my eyes should be closed—

admiring the wood-knots' swirl
that interrupted the busy nails.

The Sister Doesn't Say

that their daughter sits in the back of the class,
her hand curved like a whelk shell,
fingers working her skirt's wool,
or that a flash of satisfaction creams her eyes.

Ankles crossed, knees wide. Her silence
unravels its spool of thread down the aisle,
then she catches it again with her raised hand
and thoughtful answer.

She doesn't say that their girl pays attention straight through,
that the Sister, herself, feels a flush of disgust,
a film of dust over her own tamped desire.
That she has never met a more willfully complacent child.

What she tells the parents:
Your daughter has no friends.

When the parents ask the girl *Why?*
She answers, *They're all so boring.*

What she means:
I want myself more than I want friends.

What the girl doesn't understand is why
they want what she'd be if she were not
so strangely honest,
so unseasonably simple.

She cannot tell them
she will soon be miserable.

She'll seem to be dreaming.
She'll have brief spells of amnesia.
Only she will know what she can't remember.
The losses will accrue until she's alone,
until she knows she's other, but doesn't know why.

For years she'll hear her body
speak in tongues. Her mind will whisper
that the boy is her savior.

His hands on her benediction,
his hard penis her grace.

She'll weep at too much noise in the room.
The many confident acts by the other girls.
They will bear down on her like too much sun.

Felucca

I'd like to sail in a felucca,
and watch the buses from the hotels
empty and fill, and the far off tombs
fill and empty with their customers,
and observe someone named Jane
or Muriel or Cassie, from Miami, Boston, or
Texarkana who turns, just as she is climbing into
her air-conditioned coach, recovered from
the cost of her camel ride and the touch
of the young Egyptian with shiny eyes
whose fingers, she thinks, clutched her ribs
too tightly when she pitched out of the saddle
as the camel knelt, hissing in the sand.

She'll catch me at a distance, just my back—
the stern of my felucca wedged
between the sun-black water and the sky,
its sail gathering the dense valley air.

The scene will fall through her as the azan
falls through the bodies of the faithful.
She'll flood with a wish to unfurl,
her body silted with water light.
She'll think of the Egyptian night to come,
with moon and stars that pierce the dark
like no season she's endured since girlhood.

Because she cannot photograph the sky
or the darkness hiding her hand,
she'll photograph my boat and say,
See? This is a Felucca.
as she scrolls through the pictures of her trip.

Over zinfandels and diet Cokes her friends will peer
at the wedge of white on the noon-dark Nile—
my body a small blemish in the field.

Bottle Journal, End of Lent

Empties, they call us,
at the little shack where the sign in front reads,
Redemption, all kinds.

And we wonder which kind we'll get
when we head out to give ourselves back.
Will they welcome our collective light?

We remember how they treated Jesus—
that he refused the bitter wine
the Pharisees poured.

How they feared that clear glass
reflecting the Father. How they thought,
Break the man, break the light inside him.

When we're redeemed we'll be smashed
and our colors will bleed like a burn—
moss-green, spider-gold, chicory-blue,

shadow-red too.

Meditation on Common Ground

We share our capacity for containment.
Beyond that? One, spruce-lit mountain.
Her fat-bellied foothills' shadows stretch
westward, like game birds hung by their necks
that sway in moonlight, or the loose tongues of old men
who ride the subway cars at noon predicting apocalypse—

The wide-mouthed lapis glass, always scummy with drool.
The thick-white jug that light can't penetrate.
And the red bottle trapped among us
like a hornet caught between panes of glass,
asking which way is out.

It's true we've all been touched by the same hands—
inspected from all angles for our best reflections,
captured, like a herd of rhinos just out of a sun-black river,
tough hides aglitter in the morning light.
Astride each one, a crew of cowbirds,
unaware of the poacher and his gun.

A Brief History

Soft as moss under the pines along Beaver Dam Brook,
clear as a spring that feeds a bog, we married for love.

*

One shoulder tucked against my ribs, the sudden pop
like champagne uncorked— lips milk-blistered,

slack in sleep, you dreamt your way to me. Take my glass
heart, before the shadows spread like owls' wings.

*

He loved me. He couldn't forget that.

*

Blue baby. He saved you—
cord around your neck like a kite string.

Nurse, there's something wrong here.

Pelvic bones, tectonic plates,
sieved you into this world—

*

Here,
I give you this.

Gender Studies

When he's four my son tells me
he's had a past life.

I was a dresser, he reports.
And I had 3 drawers.

*If one of my drawers was open
I was female.*

*When all my drawers were closed
I was male.*

He doesn't say what this means,
thinks it's all been explained.

Evensong

Today the rain falls cold and fast—
bangs on my windows. Little fists.
Percussion, I say: the wind
the surging bass, the feathery snare of my husband's
breath in sleep, my snoring dog,
the steady click
of my fingers at the keyboard—

All Amens.
All Amens.

Field

1.

In the hundred-acre field of mist
that hovers above the grass,
deer graze before dawn—
button-bucks' tails flick white
in the sheer, wet silver.
Birds and crickets silenced
by the dew's weight, the coral
disk of sun just rising,
a soul suspended
over its abandoned body.

2.

On Lesbos the boats arrive
in little fleets
out of the early fog
or the solid dark night.

A small armada,
they appear on the horizon.
Their lights slip across the water,
and from the shore lights blink back.

Aphrodite gives the children
the clothes of her children.
The blue field of the Aegean
surges—the sand beneath their feet
pulled back as they step ashore.
She gives the grownups bread and tea,
the children milk and bread.
This is what it takes to tell the body,
You are here.

How You Know Where You Are

In March an oriole's nest still sways
from a bare branch—
vines and grasses matted into ropes,
the outer sack, a furred scrotum,
a downy inner bed, airy as the moon
still hanging at midmorning in the blue west.

Book Night
    for Patrick

In the Manomet branch of the Plymouth Public Library,
Mrs. Carklin stamps books and cards.
Each date shines on its yellow legend.

The open spines make boats and roof lines, a seaside village of fiction
and natural history—poetry that mounts as dates dry inside.
The cards she's pinched from each slot stack up as she teeters

the stamp first on its ink pad, then on the line.
The pencils in their holder, the telephone
in its perch, jump as she dates each book's return.

We're taking home a collision of sensibilities—
*The Case of the Black Orchid, The Book of Snakes,
The Fairie Queen*. And for you, again,

White Fang—the story of the wolf-
dog born into violence,
who kills a man to save his master.

Each time you read the story, you're saved too.

Dad comes back from buying beer,
approves each book
and pays the penny-fines.

Piled in the station wagon we ride
in and out of yellow pools of light,
our own street black as a page at night.

This is the place we'll run from—
the place we'll never stop referring to as *home*.
But tonight all we know

is the sound of snow chafing the cedars,
that we have dreams we never tell, and
that in spite of some who beat him bloody,
the brave wolf-dog will learn to love the man.

The Fold

She spins her spurs' wheels
as she oils them, listening to
wing-it, wing-it, wing-it.
Their little jingle
hits the rafters,
vibrates in the loose hay—

Wing-it-wing-it-wing-it—

If you let it be, it's that simple.

From riding out she's learned
the places hidden in the mountain
pastures—a curve or bend

like the underside of the breast,
or the fissure between scapula and rib
when the lover's back is flexed—
where, in Spring, the quail covey,
and wild ponies crop at the sparse early grass.

When her father died, she found the crease
behind his ear, where his silken scalp
formed a velvet question mark?
While he lay in the coffin,

she traced that hidden valley
with her left thumb. Anger
and tenderness rearing
inside her. All that afternoon,
the sheen of his hair's oil on her skin,
a talisman—her father-
wounded sisters unaware
of where she'd been. This morning,

in her grief, she faces the flatland.
Knowing it's there somewhere,
she rides out toward the fold.

Home Economics

Our mother writes the list on the envelope: electric bill $18.33, 100 gallons of heating oil $27.97, telephone $12.16. Cash enclosed, she calculates the change after money orders and nickel stamps. It takes two of us to pay the bills; one carries the cash and the other makes sure the first one doesn't lose it.

We learn the mysteries of finance; how money lights the drafty house which is never really warm in winter; that not-enough is a condition to be accepted, and a gallon tin of Army surplus peanut butter from the Sisters hails them as saints. We learn to say *Grace* and mean it; *Bless us oh Lord and these gifts which we are about to receive through thy bounty.*

In summer, we explore the woods behind the church and like little deer, we eat our fill of whichever berry is in season. At the beach, we slice our fingers digging clams.

When we eat pancakes spread with applesauce for dinner, she explains, we live in *genteel poverty*. And sometimes, waking late at night in my wet bed, I hear her sobbing tears that are not figured into the accounts.

Chi Lines After The Stroke

run wild in all directions.
Like a spring runoff, they riffle through the jade pivot
and florid canopy, wallow in the celestial chimney.

Shadow chi runs too.
And the blue of some lines, too bright
to take straight, makes the body's fires tilt

on twisted sheaves
along chalk-dusted trails of what's gone missing—
dove tails fluttering against the glass.

In the ICU, spice-cake becomes spice-house,
and though he knows her face, he misplaces her.

Button? Wife? Words roam his frontal lobe
until the ridge-spring channels them,
leads them out to where we wait
to hear whatever he will say.

Soon, harnessed to a nurse, he follows
the red line down the center of the hall,

and his arms reach for mine.
I'll feel the first untangling—
the way his rivers begin to remake their map.

I tell you,
his body, tilting on its altered axis,
holds me to this earth.

Farmed Out

I arrive at night and am sent to sleep
in the summer bed on the screened porch
where the day's wash, now luminous, sways over my head.
I imagine I appear, then disappear—
a child who springs from a box of shadows.

Near dawn, the Forest Hills bus begins its run along Washington.
Hiss of hydraulics, drift of diesel fumes at each stop.
Wires cat-cradle above the street.
Next morning, Peggy at her stove—
    perk, sizzle, crack.

The kettle screams.
Toast throws itself on the table.
On a plate beside my uncle's mug,
a thumb of risen cream.

I swivel my head from his face to hers
as the words push out of their mouths—
I know to laugh when my uncle laughs at his own joke.

All day fan blades slice the air into a breeze,
green tomato knobs ripen on a sill.
At dusk we eat pan-fried meat and boiled peas
beneath the Madonna on my aunt's shelf,
the mother who blesses everything,
who shares my name.

The codex in the Bible says Miriam;
means *wanted child*.

In the hall, the telephone
jumps in its cradle.
From home, the news; another—
an eleventh baby.

When it's my turn I speak to the receiver,
but my father cannot hear the question I want to ask.

The only time

my father fell into my arms
was the morning my mother died.

He was old testament—broken
in a room full of women.

As I gathered him up he cried,
I never thought she'd go first.

Then, he staggered back toward the couch
where my sisters caught him.

On the phone, the undertaker asked
how soon we'd like to see Mum's body,

while the ham she'd baked the night before
laid its mustard and brown sugar on our tongues.

House

Each dusk, I have climbed the white road
through the olive groves
to the last bend below the power lines
to stare at the three-coned trullo someone has let go.

At night, no lights open its darkness.
Shuttered windows turn back the stars.
Just as, in her last year, my mother's eyes flattened.
Caught in the camera at the registry of motor vehicles,
the starless record of her letting go.

In my mind I have made this house my mother.
I have opened the gate, righted the tumbled walls,
painted the petroglyph for joy on every cone.

Becoming

If there was going to be a birth,
I didn't know it. Like a virgin
taken in her sleep who wakes with child,

I didn't know this self in me. I turned
and saw my past strewn behind.
Like the last vestiges of old lives

the pioneers heaved out as they
prepared to climb the Great Divide,

I have rummaged through my heart;
thrown out the useless lace of shame,
regret's satin ruching. I have watched

them collapse in swale and hummock,
then burn, radiant as a prairie
fire set by a lightning flash.

Daybreak In Truro

Finally, the dark fails;
a bird breaks
the same bar over and over.
No bird calls back.

I was taught
tomorrow tells us what to do,
but I think it might be here

in each night's turning.
I have a CD of Eva Cassidy
singing *Fields of Gold*
by Sting, who took the words from Chaucer,

but the CD skips
as the song is ending,
and the words *gold-of-gold-of-gold-of-gold*
are unrelenting.   Imagine

the lovers caught
with one foot in the gilded barley,
the other in the lane,
their ardor trapped

in that unending lyric.
Before the bird, a line of flames
waist-high along the road,
its lick a wind-ripped horizon.

And you on the other side.
Not thinking, I reach out.

After Her Hip Replacement

I feel my loneliness now,
not for anyone in particular
and I'm crying in a lovely place here by the lake.
I've made some friends who make me supper
and walk with me to the end of the driveway,

as far as I'm allowed to go
on this hip which is still so delicate.
How to resist leaning for the sock on the floor—

It's her tears that mostly interest me,
the way they gurgle like a buried spring
deep in the woods, the way she has learned to let them.
A delicate weeping—almost a dew on grass
that sparkles in the black-lipped mouths of deer
as they tear, then grind the green blades in the yard.

The deer have learned not to fear
the porch screens singing in the light wind,
or the swing of the Droll Yankee and its matching swinging shadow.
They accept the thing that rocks on the wooden deck,
which comes no closer for all that motion.

Beyond the yard, the sandy street,
the smoky, tin-foil strip of lake, the fretted town beach.
She weeps again, hauling herself along the rocker's arc toward the rail.
Hips squared; one silent, one singing.

She may yet become accustomed to feasting on what's given,
may yet burn her grateful tongue on solitude's sharp beauty,
lie down at night and sleep,
one ear tuned to the wind beneath the wind,
at peace with the danger.

Change

I begin again on the far side
of something I only barely understand
as holy. Like the orange light
that drills through the west-facing windows
of the barn, spills out the other side
so the pear tree's pale green lichens glow
at sunset, and the fine ice over the grass
seems steeped in rose-hip tea.

In the long, mowed fields of midday,
where the hedgerows of autumn olive
barely shook on the winter breeze,
I saw my own body striding
like it knew where it was and who loved it—
felt the way the space between us
opened again, and closed, and opened
as simply as breathing.

Breathing

That summer, every breath trapped
halfway between mouth and lungs,
I had to reach with each
        inhalation
pull my shoulders up
        and back,
                stretch my solar plexus,
gather air like a spent elastic.

Suppertimes, we stood together in my kitchen
while I chopped onions and celery for soup.

Your task: to watch as I arranged the bulb and stalks
and bore the blade against their flesh
with the strength of my left wrist—
a fine green and white dice
accumulating on the board.

Then, with all the fingers of one fist clenched on the switch,
I'd light the stove, adjust the sip of blue flame.

And if I became distracted
by the curtains sucked against the screen,
or the sudden drone of the compressor on the ancient fridge,
you might mention I was making soup,
        might ask how long 'til dinner
might call the boys to set the table in the other room—

touch my hip,
turn me from the stove,
hold my face,
your mouth so close
I could feel
        you
breathing.

II

Water

We drink from a stone box in an ancient wall.
We drink from a copper spigot with a lion's mouth.
We drink from the Alps transported.
We drink from arches crossing valleys and rivers.
We drink from the hands of slaves nailed to crosses along the roads to Gaul.
We drink from pine woods, terraced fields, rock gorges, wind farms in the East.
We drink from city-states, their mines outside of town, their cathedrals.
We drink from each Caesar, especially Augustus in his little house.
We drink from Lydia's cruets and urns, her breasts buoyant in rose-petaled water.
We drink from palms stretched in supplication, in condemnation, in applause.
We drink from the graves of each poet and painter buried in the English Cemetery.
We drink from Senegalese illegals selling fake Pashminas on via del' Croce.
We drink from the thong shops and nail shops near the Termini.
We drink from the woman in Kenta cloth who strolls without a purse, her heels cracked
        and dusty.
We drink from the men standing, sipping— espresso, grappa, wine.
We drink from the spray-paint artist squatting on her heels on via Barbieri, who
switches out her templates as she builds her own fountain.
We drink from the flecks of green on green in the pistachio gelato, the swirl of red
        framboise.

We drink from the gypsy women begging, their babies' heads lolling on their arms.
We drink from the lights of palazzos and piazzas as dusk settles on the city.
We drink from rain-freckled streets; the red metro cars hurtling under the streets.
We drink from the tiny sparrow picking crumbs between stones at the Arch of
    Triumph.
We drink from the bride and groom who pose before the arch.
We drink from the rush of water in the shadow of the Palatine.
We wet our hands. We wet our arms. We splash our faces with the flow of Rome.
We drink.

Homesick

On the eleventh day,
I grow weary of my beloved.

She's noise in my head,
the rattle of loose

shutters I have closed
to cool my rooms.

Volgio, ho voluto, vorrò.
I want. I have wanted. I will want.

My mind objects to more
translation; can't hear

the conjugated verbs,
the *pronomi indicativi: mi*

and you in the present form;
always in the familiar.

Sex And The Soul (Sesso e l'Anima)

She: The body is a dark house
and the soul its lamp.
He: I have matches.

She: Beauty is unvisited darkness that lights within.
He: It isn't very modest is it?

She: A light shines in us but it's hard to see.
He: Try opening the shutters and the door.

She: I think of Jesus like a lover.
He: I'm not sure where that leaves me.

She: [Again] Beauty is a light.
It reaches us from inside our darkness.
He: Maybe you can look inside of me.

She: If you love Him, Jesus will live inside you.
He: Maybe you could take a look inside me.

Postcard, Vermont (Love on the Rocks c. 1898)

I thought of the year of our separation.
How we kept finding our way back—
how we seemed to be at each end of this long elastic
that wouldn't snap, but couldn't relax.

If the couple on the rock were in the middle
of the Rushing River during snowmelt,
she'd drown dressed like that.
And he'd never be able to drag her body home.

Analogy

Choke-cherries beside the brush pile
lean this way, then that, as they
discuss the wind,
like young women around the well,
whose calves flex under fluttering skirt hems
as they haul up their buckets.
April pours around them,
chilly, ham-fisted,
shutting each blossom's mouth.
Each tree, an adolescent girl
who's just discovered
how her nipples chafe against her shirt.

Last Harvest

Heirloom tomatoes fill the windowsill
over the sink: goldens, plums, and the purple
Russian Robesons (how they loved him).
The screens hum with the wind,
and sand from just-washed lettuce
forms small atolls in the sink.

At night, in our room above the kitchen,
the compressor roars
while we sleep beneath the bowed ceiling,
unaware of the crossbeam already half-cracked.
The tomatoes ripen beneath us,
the tiny island nations dissolve with the faucet's drip.

Lunches in early August are sweet slices
topped with basil and oil,
and mayonnaise dolloped on the plate.
The geese flock to Windy Meadow,
the first sign that summer is slipping.
The cooling breeze at dusk silts the fruit.
At night, you stare over my shoulder
at your reflection on the glass.

No, Don't Tell Me

Sounds come from the basement—
shuffle of moccasins on cement,
a smuggled snap and unsnap of tool boxes,
followed by a swift clink. My husband
is fixing something. His instinct for disassembling
and repair a mystery I've read for years.

In the kitchen, roasted beets cool on the pan.
Later, I'll peel the charred skins and chop them,
and then, with enough alchemy
and ingredients thrown in, they'll be soup
which we'll blow on to cool as we eat
tonight while the wind goes on gusting,

tearing the yellowwood's dead leaves off stems.
All week, the Hunter Moon
rose above the hill, a lantern glow in its shade of clouds,
until it pulled free to join the stars,
and Mars among them, close as it will be
and not again for thirty-seven years.

Hurtling south, the woodcock used the moon
for their migration, navigated
its light and shadow, object and open air
by sound and sight, as if in daylight—
then folded, each dawn, like bento boxes,
asleep in alders or hollow logs,
and at sunset, rocketed back into action;
the bayous and the live oaks
pinging their brains.

When a man (yes, a man) gets lost in the dark
and does not stop to ask directions,
he forgets he is not a woodcock
traveling toward his winter haven,
winging off planets and stars. He forgets the moon
is more than light.

The tool box cover clanks shut.
The smell of roasted vegetables has softened.
Some things are fixed for now—
as close and bright as Mars.

The Kindness of Anecdotes
(after William Stafford)

is that they let you touch
the story without commencing to think.
They plant thistles in the clover,
litter the lane with tiny birds
that wait until you're close
before they flit away.
You can watch them
and consider the lilies
who never worry, as you lift up
the drowned boy,
his red-sneakered feet splayed
on the shore, eyes not seeing the sun.
You can place him in the bluebird box nailed
to the swamp maple's trunk,
from which, each morning, he will hear how you whistle
the dog back from the field and ditch. And you?
Your heart will fold itself over him
until he is another lamination
of the darkness you carry.

Swimming Lesson

He will stand close
        but separate— ink-
stained fingers fiddling with pocket change;
having come from the presses,
through the city,
              in then out
of the Callahan Tunnel,
        straight to Logan
                to send her on her way.

Later she will wake up to see the moonrise
and notice she is not surprised
        to see she is above the clouds.
            Notice
nothing about flying amazes her,
        not the moment when she enters the white caves
not when she leaves them;
not the wild roar that settles in her spine.

But that night   when they call her flight,
and people who have been moving aimlessly in their spaces
at last lift knapsacks, shake hands,
        blow kisses, wave goodbye,
he will take her in his arms—
hold her the way the sea held her as a child.
Where, arms spread wide, hands empty,
she perfected the art of not holding on.

And for an instant man and girl
	will seem one body in that human tide
until somebody knocks or pulls at something blocked
	by their embrace. Embarrassed,
he will toss her off,
where she will sink into the crowd,
close her mouth through instinct—
surface.

All that summer he will feel
	the way his daughter slid from his arms.

III

Postcard, Sardinia

The cliffs along the coast
are covered in white thistles
and speckled with goats
whose bells sing
little syncopated songs as they cross the road
while all the cars wait
and the drivers stare at this view.

Today, I drove to the end of the road,
or, I should say,
as far as the road could take me.
There is much left alone here,
which I like.
Which I think you'd like too.

Come with me next time.
We'll drink Cannonau
(it's good for the heart).
And we'll eat goat milk pecorino.
We'll sit together above the sea
and listen as the bells pleasure the wind.

Reading Jastrun's Memorials: What the Darkness Said

The longer I wait for you oh Lord
the emptier I become,
the more to be filled.

*

Don't tell me who I am
and I won't either.
Let's both be like Pascal,
beyond saints and categories,
beyond nameable.
I am not who I say I am.
I am not who you say I am.
We were created,
which was all.

*

The ears of corn hang like questions
the knife blade cannot answer.
There is no heavenly power,
only grain and the green spruce,
only the spring rain baptizing
the morning.
Do not let your own body
blind you with its talk of death.
When you go
you take this world with you.

*

I create the mystery
in the familiar;
stars made stars by way of me.

The wolf is not the wolf,
nor the sparrow, nor the soft autumn grass,
without the swell of the moon in my body.
Understand.

Imagine another tongue,
forget the language spoken in daylight,

*

I am the keeled
sternum of the bird.
I am flight
and the chance of flight.
Even in sleep.
I am what it means to have,
always, the way up
and through
embedded in the body.

*

The words cannot hear what they say.
The gods cannot hear the words either.
Only we can hear them.
We are mud and stars.
That must be enough..

*

He asks the corn and knife,
the stars and birds,
Where are the answers?
Look to the emptiness—to the presence
around the forms.
Blake or Black Sambo,
who ever outlasts the tiger,
is living
miraculously.
And here dives the dove
and there the lamb's thorn catches,
and the earth spins its yolk.

We speak of women converted into poems by their men.
                    after reading Jack Gilbert's **Refusing Heaven**

And what does that make us feel about the men?
Strapping on the memory of their dead wives, like saddlebags
of tea from China—heaving memories with a graceful trope
across the rump of their poems after scattering ashes from the night's fire.

We hate them carrying their women like precious tea all day
as they head west across the Russian steppes. We cringe
at her brewing in some tsarist china cup in Saint Petersburg,
sipped after the long weeks of nights beside the campfire,
wolves pacing out beyond fire's light.

We will them not to tromp into the nearest bar
after currying their horse to look for an ass to caress—

We want the men to stop,
stop, stop this traipsing through rooms
in their widower's boots, clutching an image of a wife
in coitus or in the bath.
We want the him to know the her without him.

Reading The Contraband of the Hoopoe

requires a suspension of disbelief;
a new, unpredictable logic.
Also journeys,
and the sounds of bells, strings, and drums.
Bodies frozen. Bodies
in motion. Many birds,
and always the hoopoe.

Metonymies in every pocket,
sewn into the hems of travelers.
Lost ways. Old ways.
Wood, and seeds, and tenses—
carried, carry, carried, carry, carry.

The winds' ruckus through a feather's pins,
an owl's silent strike, the mute swan's splash—
departure, passage, arrival,

Regret the sieve.
Want the detritus with which
slick roads are strewn.

Relief and grief, the warp and weft
of cloth cut and stitched,
stained by golden beets,
or blackberries.

Dreams in a runnel of tongues
click and clack of black glass,
and amber beads. Also wooden beads
painted tulip-red. And beads that chatter

with spoons and candlesticks.,
How the beads are strung
declares its own language—
carried, carry, carried, carry, carry.

We Watch the International Space Station Fly Overhead

And there it goes, skipping from time to time. As bright as Venus. Our neighbors speak indistinguishable words from their patio. We assume they, too, are craning their necks to see the ISS fly. Their television set glows, and we imagine their dog, like our dog, on the couch or close to the woodstove, waiting for their masters to return inside, hang up their cold coats, and get on with the creation of leftovers.

What's amazing is that there are people in it, says my husband.

We stand together in our backyard in the dark as the ISS sails on. Her residents perhaps asleep, or testing some instrument, or maybe talking by radio to their families who are used to this situation. Could one of them be reading Carlos Santayana's claim, *Everything in nature is lyrical in its ideal essence,* contemplating the diamond light of North America's East Coast?

A century ago the coastal music would have been a daylight essence, known up close by a step across the dunes, by the sound of sea-tossed rocks, or bees drunk on lily nectar. Or by the spin of leaves stripped from their stems in hurricane winds, the roar of those winds, a rough music howling across hills and long harbors. A discord of shattered trees, loosed fishing boats smashed ashore.

Maybe someone on the ISS plays a guitar, or hums the words to *Major Tom.*

The lyricism of the natural place below gathered in the diadem of artificial light over the coast. The lyricism of their unnatural place caught in the single sunlit strobe, spun through space, star among stars, bright as the planets—here, then gone, but fixed in our minds now like a constellation that shifts each day. There, though unseeable, a light—once its match is struck, there's no unstruck.

Yankee Swap

No one tells you that sin is a gift
you can swap for wholeness.

They tell you, you must forgive
yourself, repent, change your ways,

but no one notices that sin
made it all possible,

that now, heaven awaits you
like a wrapped package on a chair.

You sit among your loved ones, know their love—
taste the water on your tongue, feel the way

your worn-out body hates the cold,
your mind tracking too many conversations,

your wife's body beside you on the couch
throwing its warmth down like an afghan

tossed across your arm in winter.
It is winter and you have this;

the love you thought you understood.
And the fear that used to wander

has settled at your feet.
You have the new year you may not live through,

an ember some god is blowing on
with round, hard cheeks—her hands

a funnel around her lips building a fire in you.
I see it as you rise, confused,

exhausted. You turn and turn among your sisters

and other loves—preparing
to swap the gift that doesn't fit

The Sudden Tremendous Weight

of rain in the chokecherry
in July cracks a limb
that will take a day
to break down to brush
and next year's stove wood.

We'll need the sawhorse
for the larger branches,
the barrow to transport
wood to the shed—heavy gloves
to stave off splinters.

On a cool morning
with cloudy skies we begin—
lightening
with each pass of the saw's blade.

Conjugation

After a shared bath
you powder my thighs.

I think of the brace of oxen at the fair.
How they bowed together to take the yoke,

heart-shaped faces lifting
as the ox-man set the hitch—

hauled stone through mud

Head bowed, your shoulders curve below my breasts
as you dust my flesh with Blue Chintz talcum.

If you asked me at this moment
what the ox wants most

I'd say, the twinned curves of the yoke—
the scratch of the ox-man's switch.

The Little Lights

At the olive oil museum
we are ushered down
a wide slope into semi-darkness
to see the pressing stones
that fill the center of the cave—
the worn rut cut by boys
sold to the monks each year—
who dragged the top stone around
across the bottom stone
to grind the fruit—fragrant liquid,
of the Salento's world
pouring into vessels.
A blade of the midday sun
falls just outside the door.

Flies accompany us on our tour
buzzing over the damp, earthen berms
where the pressers slept in shifts
on piles of hay—children
who lived underground all season,
unless taken by the monks for prayer, or
whose rags got caught between the stones
and were carried away.

In the remains of the monastery's church
the fresco of the Crucifixion's worn
to a haze, the blood of the final wound
faded, a pink as pale as a newborn's sole.

Life Inside and Out: A Cento
for Linda Gregg

Backing away, I am pleased.
Because this world matches
my life inside and out—
the dark thing hardly visible.

If you came and saw me now
you might remember how glad I was.
I climbed the mountain.
Ascended steps the moon had already taken.

I bring no sad stories to warn the heart.
All the flowers are matured this year.
The cloth over the broken window
swells and goes flat, and swells again.

I see women everywhere seeking a love that changes.
I will not stop looking for Song and Color.
If love does not reign, we are unsuited
for the season of ripeness.

Perhaps my happiness proves a weakness
In my life, even my failures please me.
I hear bells and discern the silvery-gray
backs of sheep grazing in moonlight.

We are tokens of what is.
A breeze.   Billows.   The doorway curtain.
I am putting myself together—
alone and happy.

Notes:

The term "old testament" as used, comes from E. Ethelbert Miller

A cento is a poem comprised of lines or phrases from another source. All of the words used in "Life Inside and Out" are from poems included in Linda Gregg's *In the Middle Distance* (Graywolf Press, 2006)

ABOUT THE AUTHOR

Miriam O'Neal's poems and reviews have appeared in many journals, including *AGNI, Blackbird Journal, Cathexis, The Guide Book, The North Dakota Review,* and elsewhere. Her collection, *We Start With What We're Given,* was published by Kelsay Books in 2018. She is a 2019 Pushcart Prize nominee, as well as having earned honorable Mention in the 2019 Princemere Poetry Prize, and being a Notable Poet in the 2019 Disquiet International Poetry Competition. She lives in Plymouth, MA.

CPSIA information can be obtained
at www.ICGtesting.com
Printed in the USA
FSHW010332090620
70575FS